DAMIAN HERNANDEZ

Born Great

Unlock Your Power and Greatness

Discover your true abilities, skills, and unlimited potential to make great things happen in your life.

Born Great

ISBN: 9781733829366

Editor: Theastarr Valerie - Empress Royále Publishing

Cover Design: Empress Royále Publishing

Photographer: Marcus Salvary: Photo World (Trinidad and Tobago)

Title Page: "Mountains" from *Birgl* (pixabay.com)

Empress Royále Publishing

"Everything tells a story; let us help you tell your story to the world."

Email: empressroyalepublishing@gmail.com

For Speaking Engagements:

Damian Hernandez
Phone Number: 1-868-781-5313
Email: dp-hernandez@hotmail.com

ACKNOWLEDGMENT

To My Family. My beautiful wife, Candice. My son, Damarian. My daughter, Damaiyah. You inspire me to live a purpose driven life. My success is all thanks to your support. I love my family.

To My Mother, Gloria Hernandez. Thank you for your hard working attitude. You ensured that I was always well taken care of. Thank you for the example that you've set for my sisters (Denise and Rhona) and I.

To My Other Sisters, Gemma and Marscia Merdin. Thank you for your support.

To My Father. Thank you for changing your life and being the great man that you are today.

Robbie and Shishma Mohammed. Thank you for being our friends and personal mentors. You coached us on how to build our business for financial independence. Your life is an example to many others and you're always willing to help. You're such an awesome couple.

Empress Royále Publishing. Thank you Ms. Valerie for helping and assisting me in getting this book published.

ABOUT THE AUTHOR

Damian Hernandez is a young inspiring motivational speaker and an independent business owner. He loves talking to people, especially youths. He began speaking to students in primary and secondary schools about having dreams, goals, vision, respect, finding their purpose, how to succeed, and the importance of prayer.

He's very passionate about helping others become successful and financially independent. Because he understands helping people is one of the major parts of success.

Damian has a great work ethic, is purpose driven, enthusiastic about life, and is continuously developing a positive mindset. He is also funny and loves the Lord, his personal savior, Jesus Christ.

Damian and his wife Candice are the CEOs of **D.C.D.D Enterprises**. Their network marketing business was launched in February 2020. Damian is constantly learning, growing, and developing himself into an entrepreneur. His leadership skills allow him to help others live successfully.

As Damian begins to move across Trinidad and Tobago, the Caribbean, and other countries, his desire is to continue to impact others, teaching them the principles of success.

With God as the priority, anyone can be successful. When you do get the opportunity to hear him speak, your outlook on life will change. You wouldn't be satisfied with going back to a life of mediocrity.

He is a cricket lover who plays for **Canefarm Cricket Sports Club**, a Trinidad based cricket club. He loves reading, singing, writing, listening to highly successful people, and being around like-minded individuals.

Prior to his epiphany, Damian had been living a life of failure. He remembers being told that he would ***constantly fail*** as a man, husband, and father. And he wouldn't be successful in life. All of these things were stirred up inside him to prove people wrong: that he can live his best life achieving his dreams. There was a point in his life that he started to wonder if all he heard from the naysayers were true. He cried, sucked up all the pain and forgave all who hurt him. In was at that point he made a decision to make great things happen in his life.

Nevertheless, Damian found his gifts and he is pursuing it. He inspires, encourage, and uplift people to live their best life no matter what the circumstances are. Damian changed his mindset, associates, and the way he did things. Now his **FOCUS** is on his goals and developing himself mentally to achieve greatness.

INTRODUCTION

Do you know the reason why you were born great? *You were born to achieve great things.*

"Some people are born into power
Others ***work*** for it
Others are forced to accept it
Some achieve greatness"

You were designed for greatness!

I believe everyone in this world can become successful once they believe. I am an independent business owner and motivational speaker. One of my main goals is to talk to as much people as I can, because they need to hear my message. I was created to impact others.

This book has some of the basic ideas and concepts to achieve your goals, dreams, and to bring out your limitless power. The information will give you encouragement and inspire you to succeed. After you read this book, it is up to you to apply the information to your life and embrace the process to your destiny.

I'm not inspired just to live; I'm inspired to make a difference in people's lives. You have unlimited potential to live out your dreams.

You can accomplish anything you want.

You can:

- Make **ANY** amount of money
- Live in the house of your dreams
- Own and drive any car(s) you want
- Take a trip to all the countries on your bucket list
- Take a vacation

All these things are available to you. I know you can have it...

It's POSSIBLE.

I was born in Trinidad and Tobago. I grew up in a place called Arima, located on the east side of Trinidad. My parents were living an average lifestyle; ***paycheck*** to ***paycheck***. They struggled to pay bills and barely made ends meet. I was raised in a house with my two sisters: Denise and Rhona.

When I was younger, I didn't know what I wanted for my life. Eventually, I realized what was going on with my parents. As I grew older, I began to think,
I was not created by God to live an average life of struggle forever...

I know what life has to offer. I've discovered the reason for my existence. Going through pain is a ***temporary*** thing.

It is not meant to stay.
It is part of life.
It is something we have to go through.

The pain and struggles we go through in life is part of the process. Gaining knowledge, wisdom, understanding, and educating myself on how to succeed, was the ***greatest*** thing I ever did.

In this book I'm going to share with you how you can work towards your vision and live in your purpose.

Enjoy it and blessings in all your future endeavors.

God bless you.

Damian Hernandez

"Not everybody can be famous, but everybody can be great. Greatness is determined by service."

Martin Luther King Jr.

"The most important thing is to try to inspire people so that they can be great in whatever they do."

Kobe Bryant

Table Of Contents

Chapter One

What You Think About Is What You'll Bring About

Your brain is very powerful. God created you with a brain to think great, awesome, and wonderful things. Start your day with positive affirmations.

For example, start off your day by saying:

Great things are going to happen today.

Focus on the good things. Change negative self-talk into positive self-talk. How you start your morning determines the rest of your day.

When you wake up late, you panic. Immediately you create a narrative that nothing good will happen for the rest of the day. Why? Your day started with a negative emotion and a cynical view which carries into the balance of your day.

Instead of letting these thoughts control you, start your day with positive affirmations like,

Today will be a great day.

I'm going to have an awesome day.

Your day will certainly improve.

"For as he thinks in his heart, so is he..."
Proverbs 23:7

A man is what he thinks. Remember what you think about, is what you'll bring about. You need to understand the importance of the way you think about life, success, accomplishing your dreams and goals, becoming an entrepreneur, etc.

Train your brain to think differently. Reframe your thought patterns.

Thinking things like, *"this won't work,"* or *"I'm so foolish"*, doesn't contribute to a healthy mindset. If you want to change your life, you have to change the way you think.

If you change the way you think, you will then change the way you perceive life. And if your thoughts are positive and constructive, and if you act on them faithfully, you will achieve greatness.

What you *think* > is what you'll *say*

What you *say* > is what you'll *do*

What you do on a *continual basis* > becomes a *habit*

Your *habits* > creates your *character*

Your *character* > determines your *destiny*

Everything that you see in this world begins with a ***thought***.

When I was young, my way of thinking was negative. I had no positive thoughts about my life. Achieving success did not cross my mind.

My way of thinking has changed. I've developed a healthy thought pattern and mindset.

I realized that your thoughts manifest in the physical.

A contributing factor for my positive self-esteem comes from surrounding myself with people who have an optimistic mindset. I also read inspirational books that promote self-development.

Why do you think a majority of people are living a mediocre life? Living in poverty? Or living an average lifestyle? Someone first had that thought and their thoughts have manifested.

How can they come out of this average thinking?
By changing their thought patterns.

Changing the way you think, changes the way you live.

Have a positive mindset towards life and you will see how things shape differently.

Mindset is a settled way of thinking; our thoughts are established through experiences, education, and things that we've learnt. There are patterns that shape our lives and the way we live.

Unless you change your thoughts, you would never change your reality. The issue is the way you think of your problems. If you alter your thought patterns and develop solutions, your problems would be history.

That's why it is best for you to be a solution seeker rather than a problem finder. God planted the seed of greatness within you when He created you. God created each one of us to live an abundant life, a life of prosperity, wealth, non-stop blessings; a life where we can achieve our dreams and goals.

He has plans for you, and He has already put your purpose in you. We were created for greatness, not mediocrity.

You want to be successful? *You have to be successful in mind before you could become successful in life.*

Do you have the courage to think? If you can think, you can change, move, evolve, and grow. You are ***one*** thought away from your greatest idea.

Thoughts become reality.

It all **begins** with the brain.

The idea that you have in your mind, bring it out to show the world what you have to offer; no matter what people may think, say, or do. You were given that idea to help conquer this world and live the life you've always dreamed of. Begin to guard your mind against negative programing; you are in charge of what you put into your brain.

Start filtering your thoughts. If you don't program your mind, it will be programmed.

Guard your thoughts.

There are ***no*** limitations to your mind. Whatever you have in your thoughts will materialize.

"Wherever you focus your attention, wherever you put your energy that is what will grow. If you focus on the good that you want, you welcome abundance, prosperity, and success."
~Mark Fisher

We have to monitor our thoughts very close. Henry Ford once said, *"Whether you think you are great or not, you are absolutely correct."*

"We have the power to control our thoughts. Before we can accumulate riches in great abundance, we must magnetize our minds with intense desire for riches."
~Napoleon Hill

Your thoughts are responsible for everything that happens to you. Behavior is influenced by your predominant thoughts and attitude. They control your actions and reactions. As your thoughts are, so is your life.

Think positively and with direction. If you are not thinking with direction, your mind is running wild. Focus on the best for your life.

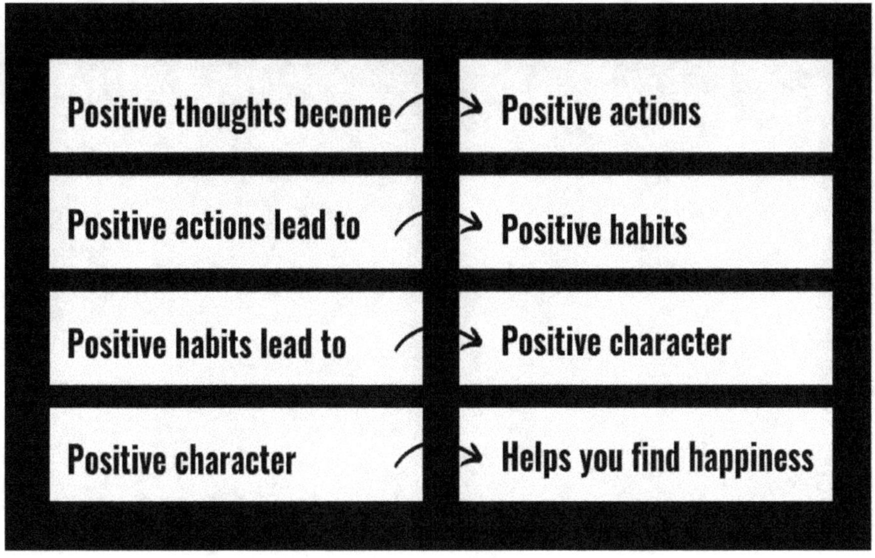

Chapter Two

Speak What You Want: The Power Of Words

The previous chapter ties into this chapter. In order to get what you want, you have to speak it over your life. The words that you speak or the things that you talk about can come into existence.

Learn and train yourself to speak *great, awesome, wonderful, good, success, positivity, prosperity, riches,* and *wealth* over your life because it can surely become a reality.

The words that exit out of your mouth are very crucial. Words are very powerful. Your words have power and energy. We should be mindful of the way we speak and the things we speak about. It shows our true character.

Be *careful* of what you say to yourself or to others. Your words can make or break another person. So choose your words wisely.

The saying *"THINK BEFORE YOU SPEAK"* is absolutely true. People can say things to hurt themselves or others.

It's best to say things to encourage, uplift, and motivate people.

Tell someone, **"You were born to live your greatest life ever. You can do it! It's possible that you can live your dream."**

But in most cases, people prefer to say negative things about others. These words are discouraging. Telling someone, "*your life has no meaning,*" is detrimental to their development.

Sometimes you may be the only source of encouragement that you have.

I also discovered that when someone is down and out, struggling, or going through pain, it's because they talk about their current state or past experiences.

I want to let you know this... **STOP** talking about where you are in your life right now. Instead, speak to your future.

Focusing on or talking about the past and your current state, keeps you from progressing. Don't put your time and energy in the ***here and now***, look to the future.

Avoid speaking about the things that you have, but don't want.
Speak about the things that you want, but don't have.

Why do you think that a vehicle only has three rearview mirrors?

The left rearview mirror is small.

The right rearview mirror is small.

The interior rearview mirror is small.

Yes, the rearview mirrors are used for **reversing**.

But most of the times while driving, you don't spend time looking at the rearview mirror to see what's behind you. The time is spent looking through the windshield. That's because you're looking at where you are heading... towards your destiny.

It's the same way that you have to operate when looking at your dreams. Keep speaking about the things that you want to accomplish in your life.

As I matured, I realized that my vocabulary was affected by my environment. The people I used to speak to and the conversations that I had, was inferior. They did not contribute to my development into a successful man.

I've changed my associates and started to be around like-minded individuals; people who speak positively and uplift others.

Your life will move in the direction of your words.

"Death and life are in the power of your tongue: and they that love it shall eat the fruit thereof."
Proverbs 18:21

You are planting seeds when you talk. At some point you're going to ***eat*** that fruit. Words are like seeds. When you speak something out, you give life to what you are saying.

In other words, you can't plant pumpkin seeds and expect to sow *watermelons*. You are going to reap the fruit from the seeds you've been sowing. Make sure you're planting the right seeds.

You can't talk *defeat* and expect *victory*

You can't speak *negative* and expect to have a *positive life*

If you speak poverty, you're going to have a life of poverty.

POSITIVE SPEECH: DAILY AFFIRMATIONS

- I'm **blessed** and **highly favored**
- I'm **above** and not beneath
- **Blessings** shall **flow upon me**
- *If God be for me who can be against me*
- *No weapon formed against me shall prosper*
- I'm a **winner**
- I'm an **overcomer**
- I'm a **conqueror**
- I will *live my dreams*
- I will **succeed**

- I am **great**

Speak victory over your life

Speak positive things in your life

You are great

There's greatness within you

You deserve the best for your life because there is a bright future in you that needs to be released.

"For assuredly, I say to you, whoever says to this mountain, 'Be removed and be cast into the sea,' and does not doubt in his heart, but believes that those things he says will be done, he will have whatever he says."
Mark 11:23

Use your words wisely.

Words have the power to heal and uplift. Your words have the ability to change lives. When you speak what you want you can change things in your life.

Speak to yourself every day.

Declare prosperity over your life because you were born to prosper. It is time to change the way you speak about yourself.

If you speak bad things to yourself, you invite bad things into your life.
If you speak great things to yourself, you invite great things into your life.

Stop doubting yourself. You **CAN DO IT!**

If you have a great business opportunity in your hands, speak it into your life.

YES, you CAN speak it into your life.

You CAN have it.

YES YOU CAN!

Chapter Three

Believe In Yourself

Sometimes, in going through the process of pursuing your dreams, there is a voice inside, telling you things to distract you, or to even try to put doubt in your mind. That voice says, "*YOU CAN'T DO IT.*"

DON'T listen to that inner voice.

If you're hearing that voice; it came to kill, steal, and destroy.

Stand strong, believe in yourself, and chase your dreams.

Once you believe in yourself, anything is possible. Believing in yourself firmly and strongly makes you **unstoppable**.

Because of your drive and determination to go after your dreams, nothing can step in your way. Once you believe that you can be successful, everything is possible.

We all face problems. But, when you focus on the solution, you will be successful. It takes a lot of courage to believe in yourself, but you have the willpower to do whatever it takes to get the job done.

Do you want to be happy and successful? *It's your responsibility to make it happen, by applying the knowledge I'm sharing in this book.*

The decisions and choices you make for your life will determine where you end up in the future. Make the right choices for your life so that you won't live in regret.

Your life is yours.

You must decide how to invest in your life. You are responsible for everything that takes place in your life. Invest in something worthwhile.

Whatever that *something* is, you have to picture yourself there; see it in your mind before it manifests in the physical.

Do you see yourself…

- ☐ *Opening a business?*
- ☐ *Building a hospital?*
- ☐ *Becoming a football player?*
- ☐ *Becoming a cricket player?*
- ☐ *Becoming a basketball player?*
- ☐ *Being an athlete?*
- ☐ *Opening a restaurant?*
- ☐ *Opening a salon?*
- ☐ *Becoming a networking marketer?*

Whatever gifts God put in you when you were created, just BELIEVE.

God created each person with gifts. We all are gifted and you have to figure out what your gifting is.

How do you discover your gift? *Your gift is the thing that you do at your absolute best with the least amount of effort; your gift is actually trapped inside of you.*

In other words, your future is not ahead of you, it is WITHIN you.

That thing that you love to do is your gift.

The thing that you're talented in is your gift. Believe and trust in God for the things that He has in store for you.

"A man's gift makes room for him, and brings him before great men."
Proverbs 18:16

- You were born great.

- Believe in yourself.

- Believe in God to reveal your gift.

Find out from God why you were born. When you learn what your gift is, start pursuing it.

When you do what you love, and you love what you do, you will succeed your whole life through. You weren't designed to go to a job and be there for forty to forty five years and retire broke.

THIS IS ONE THING I WANT YOU TO BELIEVE.

I will share more about this in a later chapter.

Know your worth, believe in your ability.

YOU ARE SOMEBODY!

Don't allow anybody to make you feel inferior. It is **POSSIBLE** that you can live your dreams. This is your moment ***right now***, not tomorrow, or next year.

Your time to shine is NOW!

ENOUGH PROCRASTINATION!

Stop keeping yourself from moving forward.

Your time is one of the most powerful tools you have.

Successful people don't waste time. The reason some people are very successful is because they've acknowledged the value of TIME.

This is the time for your breakthrough.

The time to change your life is NOW.

Whatever you believe and conceive you can achieve.

BELIEVE

BELIEVE

Stop stressing, stop worrying and start believing in yourself. Success is personal. No one will believe in you except... **you**.

We need to take control of our mind and our emotions. Once you can conquer your mind you can conquer anything around you. You have to manifest your destiny. No one can do that for you. Stand bold and brave.

In life you have to be bold. Challenges, circumstances, and obstacles will all be thrown at you. Friends or family members may tell you negative things like, *"You can't do it."*

Don't allow those things to stop you from believing in yourself. There will always be **DOUBTERS**...

continue to believe in yourself. There are ***dream stealers***... believe in yourself.

People on your job may tell you that your dream doesn't make any sense and it won't work out for you because they don't have a vision. Those people on your job can't see what you see because it was placed in *your* mind and in your spirit from God.

Only those who can see the invisible can do the impossible.

What people may think or feel is impossible for them, it's possible for you.

With God ALL things are possible.

Your belief can shape what happens in the future. As you go through life day by day, believe in yourself and in God for your dreams. Just know this: things are going to come your way that you didn't expect to come, but God will definitely take care of you through the process.

You have to fight for what you want for your life. It's not going to come just like that. Keep going. Keep chasing after your destiny.

The only person to believe in you is ***you***. Your determination and willpower will take you where you want to go.

Going through the process of becoming successful, you have to face failures. Failure is the stepping stone to success; failure is a massive part of being successful. So get comfortable going through some failure in life.

There is no shortcut to success, you have to go through the failure, whether you like it or not. Only those who dare to fail greatly can ever achieve greatly. Make the decision to take action to prove people wrong about the negative things they've been saying about you, or to you. They'll try to discourage and criticize you just because you are making your life better.

People are going to come at you. Do you know what I call these people? *HATERS!*

Just because you are doing your best to be the great person that you're created to be, because you are success driven and running towards your dreams, some people will ***hate*** you. And sometimes you don't know how to handle it.

"When you pass through the waters, I will be with you; and through the rivers, they shall not overflow you. When you walk through the fire, you shall not be burned, nor shall the flame scorch you.
For I am the Lord your God, The Holy One of Israel, your Savior."
Isaiah 43:2-3

When you are under attack, God will fight your battles for you. Believe in yourself. MOST IMPORTANTLY, believe in God and put **all** your trust and faith in Him.

What's the difference between a winner and a loser?

WINNERS	LOSERS
VS	
- Make Things Happen	- Make Excuses
- Grind	- Whine
- Have Dreams	- Have Schemes
- Work Hard	- Are Lazy
- Are Positive	- Are Negative
- See the gain	- See the pain
- Get back up when they fall down	- Stay down when they fall

Winners fall down numerous times and continue to get back up. Winning isn't about not getting knocked down, winning is about getting back up, dusting yourself off, and moving towards your dreams.

A quote from Sydney J. Harris about winners and losers states that, *"A winner knows how much he still has to learn, even when he is considered an expert by others; a loser wants to be considered an expert by others before he has learned enough to know how little he knows."*

Don't settle into a comfort zone, and don't let success go to your head. Enjoy your success briefly, and then move on. Greatness lies ahead.

"For a righteous man may fall seven times, and rise again."
Proverbs 24:16

Develop a winner's mindset and you will win. You were born to win because you were ***BORN GREAT.***

Chapter Four

Be Fearless And Have Faith

"For God has not given us a spirit of fear; but of power and of love and of a sound mind."
2 Timothy 1:7

"Fear not, for I have redeemed thee; I have called you by your name; you are Mine."
Isaiah 43:1

When you were born, you were born with only two fears: falling and a loud sound. All other fears are irrelevant.

Fear is:

False
Evidence
Appearing
Real

There is nothing to be afraid of in terms of pursuing your purpose. The only thing you should be fearful of is *fear itself*. When you are running towards your dreams, have no fear. Be bold and courageous.

FEAR NOTHING!

You have the spirit of entitlement to do whatever it takes for as long as it takes to accomplish your dreams. Don't allow fear to take control of your life.

Fear:

- Kills your hopes and dreams
- Can put you in the hospital
- Ages you
- Can paralyze you
- Can keep you from doing what you're supposed to do

You have to overcome the fear in life. When you face your fears, you will become the person you're meant to be. When you face your fears, you become more powerful.

Fear is of the devil and produces death; faith is of God and produces life. Your fear is always about that which does not exist.

How can you overcome your fears? *Focus on the reason* ***WHY*** *you want to achieve your dreams.*

Your "WHY" will push you towards your vision so you can act out in faith and bring life to your dreams. The people who are living their dreams are the ones that had the courage to overcome their fears.

Fear is the voice of the *average*; you must kill your fears. The only way you can change your life is to step into your fear.

You have to do that thing you fear most.

You have to do whatever it takes to conquer fear.

Your largest fear carries your greatest growth.

You are bigger than your fear.

Fear has no place in your heart; fear will not stop you once your *desire* to win is strong enough.

FEAR NOTHING AT ALL!

What you *should* be afraid of, is:

- Living a mediocre life
- Having an average lifestyle
- Quitting on your dreams

Push through the pain and conquer your biggest fear. Look in the mirror and tell that person *I won't be stopped because of fear*.

You are God's divine creation. Trust in God and believe in Him for great things to come.

There is a divine precept in you

↓

Sealed up waiting to break free

One point in my life, I had to step out to take action, have self-confidence, motivation, and the will to succeed. It took courage for me to have faith in myself and God, to push through all my past experiences. I was not going to allow my past to dictate what God planned for my future. If I had allowed my past to dictate my future, I would not have been able to accomplish anything.

I have faith now, believing that everything is going to work out for the best.

Faith is trusting God even when you don't understand His plan.

Faith is confidence in what we hope for and assurance about what we do not see.

We live by faith and not by sight.

Your faith produces perseverance.

"No matter what has happened to you in the past or what is going on in your life right now, it has no power to keep you from having an amazingly good future if you will walk by faith in God. God loves you! He wants you to live with victory over sin so you can possess His promises for your life today!"

~Joyce Meyer

"Therefore I say to you, whatever things you ask when you pray, believe that you receive them, and you will have them."

Mark 11:24

"Your faith should not stand in the wisdom of men but in the power of God."
1 Corinthians 2:5

If you're going through pain, stress, problems, challenges, or any kind of adversity, don't give up. Don't give in or throw in the towel. You don't know what's going to happen in your life, it could be a very painful situation, but you have to step out in faith.

Having faith is knowing everything is awaiting you on the other side.

Faith is such a simple word, but it's ***not*** easy. The reason that faith isn't easy is because we've got to have faith to believe in God. Hebrews 11:6 says, *"Without faith it is impossible to please Him..."*

Faith says that you must believe in God's power and His presence in your life. Without faith, no man shall receive anything; a man with doubt shall receive ***nothing***.

The difference between a dream and a destiny is that a dream is just a wish, but a destiny has faith in it.

Don't worry about anything that may challenge you in life, God **WILL** see you through. Focus on believing in yourself and don't worry about the doubters. You have to be ready to live your best life, your dreams, and to live beyond your comprehension. Just don't lose faith.

Faith doesn't equal *easy.*

Faith equals *possibility.*

It is an expectation that something will happen, even when you don't see it. *Faith is the substance of things hoped for, the evidence of things not seen (Hebrews 11:1).*

Faith is an ***action*** word. It is the words that you speak and the action you take.

You have to believe it before you achieve it.

It doesn't matter who you are, or where you've been, if you have faith and the desire to succeed, you can accomplish anything.

Keep your head up. Success doesn't come from giving up or quitting, it comes from dreaming and believing that you can get through anything if you set your mind to it.

POSITIVE SPEECH: DAILY AFFIRMATION

I WILL NOT QUIT UNTIL I'M LIVING THE LIFE I DREAM OF!

Chapter Five

Don't Ever Quit, Don't Give Up

"One of the most common causes of failure is the habit of quitting when one is overtaken by temporary defeat."
~Napoleon Hill

Quitting or giving up on your dreams should never be an option. In your life you will have two choices: ***Go Forward*** or ***Give Up***.

Before you think about giving up, keep in mind that giving up means that your dreams and goals will never happen.

That is the guarantee of quitting.

No matter the circumstances, PLEASE don't give up on your dreams.

God will always make a way where there seems to be no way. Although the process may be hard at times, you have to understand that **HARD WORK** is part of life.

You're tired?

You don't want to get out of bed?

Do you feel like throwing in the towel?

Is the process too much to handle?

No matter how you feel…

Get up ✓

Dress up ✓

Show up ✓

Never give up ✓

Talk to yourself every day.

POSITIVE SPEECH: DAILY AFFIRMATION

I will fight!

I will not give up!

I will reach my goal!

NOTHING can stop me!

Life has a special meaning for those who are running towards their dreams. In the process of working on your dream, you are going to experience some failure, set back, disappointments, pain, and defeats.

In the process of doing that, you will discover some things about yourself that you didn't know existed.

You have greatness within you

You are powerful

You are greater than your circumstances

It is necessary to work and develop yourself. Surround yourself with like-minded individuals; those who've already accomplished their goals. Separate yourself from those who are not contributing to your success. The people who you associate yourself with determine who you are.

Birds of a feather flock together.

Hang around losers > you will end up a loser

Hang around winners > you will be a winner

Do you want to be successful? Hang around successful people.

Isolate yourself from energy drainers and dream stealers. Associate yourself with men and women who have good character.

Bad company corrupts good character.

90% of your success is being around successful people. Be around people who dream big.

"And let us not grow weary while doing good, for in due season we shall reap if we do not lose heart."
Galatians 6:9

"For I know the thoughts that I think toward you, says the Lord, thoughts of peace and not of evil, to give you a future and a hope."
Jeremiah 29:11

Never give up on what you're doing.

Never stop believing.

Never give up.

No matter how hard things get, stick to your dreams. Your day will come. All of your hard work will pay off.

If success was easy everybody would do it.

Everybody has dreams and goals, but it is very important to write your WHY down.

WHY do you want to be successful?

WHY do you want to achieve your dreams?

WHY do you want to have a great lifestyle?

WHY do you want to separate yourself from the masses?

WHY?

WHY?

WHY?

The reason **WHY** I'm on the journey to success is because I can't let my son, daughter, or my wife, experience the things I've been through. I have to do this to make my family happy.

My children must be proud of their daddy; my wife must be happy and proud of me. I don't want my family to face the struggles, pain, adversity, or any kind of suffering. I'm creating a culture where my family can live in wealth.

The statement I'm about to make is for the men...

> We as men have to take care of our wives and children. The society we live in has painted a distorted picture of fatherhood; one where men shy away from their responsibilities. We need to **MAN UP**, take care of our responsibilities, and do what God expects us to do as **men**.

I'm building a legacy for my family and future generations.

"A good man leaves an inheritance to his children's children."
Proverbs 13:22

You can't buy a legacy; it is something that you earn. I **CANNOT** let my wife, son, or daughter down. This is the reason **WHY** I'm in the process of living my dream.

What is *your* **WHY**?

Your **WHY** lets you know that you can't:

- Give up
- Quit
- Give in
- Throw in the towel
- Stop

Your **WHY** drives and motivates you to push toward your dreams. Make sure you have your **WHY** crystal clear in your mind. It will help you face any kind of trial or tribulation.

FOCUSING ON THE WHY 101:

- There's no time for foolishness
- Strive towards greatness
- You're on a mission heading towards your destiny

"Once you're running after your destiny, you will automatically distance yourself from your history."
~T.D. Jakes

You won't have time to think about your past failures and experiences. Leave your past in the past because your future is most important.

Quitting or giving up on your dreams was never an option.

Chapter Six

Prayer Is Very Important

"But seek first the kingdom of God, and His righteousness, and all these things shall be added to you."
Matthew 6:33

What are all these *things*? *Your gifts, your dreams and everything that your heart desire.*

All these things God has in store for you, it's already planted within you to bring it out in this world.

"Trust in the Lord with all your heart,
And lean not on your own understanding;
In all your ways acknowledge Him,
And He shall direct your paths."
Proverbs 3:5-6

It is very important to begin your day with God, the Creator of all things. Have a relationship with God and involve Him in your business, so you can be prosperous. God wants you to be successful and live abundantly, but you **CANNOT** do it without Him. We should dedicate our lives to God, daily.

"To You, O Lord, I lift up my soul."
Psalm 25:1

Every morning when we go before God, we need to ask Him to ***show us*** our assignments. Allow Him to take control over your day. Choose to fellowship with God daily. Walk with God for life. God must be first priority in your life.

God says, *what's most important is that you must get to know me*.

The first thing you must do when you wake up in the morning is talk to God. Invite God into your daily experiences, so you can have successful days.

Prayer should be a habit, but for most people prayer is an occasional surprise or when things are falling apart.

Pray no matter what; in the good times and the bad times. God will see you through your situation or whatever struggles you are faced with in life. Even if you forget to acknowledge Him, He will never leave you or forsake you, because *God loves you*, you are *His creation*, you are *His child*.

He can do anything for you once you have a relationship with Him and pray every day.

Some people say God doesn't answer their prayers. What we need to understand is that He does not operate in our timing, but His.

God's timing is always the best time.

Sometimes He shows up when you least expect it, you just have to prepare yourself for His blessings upon your life. You have to understand God is God because ***EVERYTHING IS POSSIBLE*** with Him. There is nothing hard for God. He can do **ALL** things.

I can do ALL things through Christ who strengthens me.

This book highlights the steps to success, how to live your dream, and accomplish your goals, so that you can have a wonderful lifestyle.

Everybody wants to be happy and successful.

If you don't want to be happy and successful, something must be wrong.

Once you want to be happy and successful you **CANNOT** do it without God.

Do you know why you can't succeed without God? *Because I tried it already and it didn't work out.*

Accepting Jesus Christ as my personal Lord and savior has been the best decision I ever made.

I had some things going for me. God placed opportunities in my life to succeed, great business opportunities where I was making a substantial amount of money, and I was very thankful for it. I feel good about all the great things that have happened in my life.

God had showed me the way to success because I made the decision to have Him in my life. What I should have done instead, was make the decision once in my life and manage that decision for the rest of my life.

The mistake came when I took my eyes off Christ.

- I shifted my focus to things of this world.

- I forgot to pray.

- I leaned on my own understanding.
- I thought I was invincible.

I learned that when you ask God for what you want and receive the blessings, you need to be ***thankful***, ***grateful***, and give God ***praise***.

When you take your focus off God, stop communicating with Him, or stop praying, you risk losing all the blessings. You can trickle back to a former mediocre life or even worse.

Don't ever stop praying because God knows what's best for you.

You CANNOT succeed without God.

Without prayer, it is going to be difficult for your dreams to become a reality.

Prayer is more than talking to God. It is a powerful *act of worship* that glorifies God and highlights our need for Him. When prayer becomes a lifestyle, we respond to Jesus' redemptive work of salvation. Prayer connects us to the source and purpose of our existence.

Picture your life without food and water; picture yourself without taking care of your physical health.

Your body needs food, water, and exercise to build a proper structure to live and grow. Your **spirit** needs *prayer* and the <u>word of God</u> to build a proper structure to live and grow. So take care of your spiritual health as well. Feed your spirit with the word of God for knowledge and wisdom on how to obey God's principles, fulfilling purpose.

Prayer should reflect the relationship we have with God. After all, it is beautiful to think that we have been given the ability to communicate with Him. In any moment and from any place, we can thank Him, ask for His strength, discern His will and become more like Christ.

"Draw near to God and He will draw near to you."
James 4:8

God knows there is an enemy out there who hates and wants to destroy you.

Satan doesn't want you to succeed. The devil doesn't like you. He is trying to keep you away from your destiny. The enemy hates when a man walks with God. He does not want you to become the person God created you to be.

God wants you to hook up with Him so He can help you take care of yourself. He's going to help you deal with the enemy, because God is going to give you the power to take care of everything that you need.

Live with God

Obey God

All we have to do is follow God's plan and purpose for our lives.

The enemy also has plans too, but you have to move with God's plans. God has already worked it all out; He knows the end from the beginning.

Those who leave everything in God's hands will eventually see God's hands in everything.

In 2015, Denzel Washington addressed a graduating High School class, encouraging the students with these words, *"Anything that you're doing which is good, the number one thing is to PUT GOD FIRST."*

He highlighted how important it is to have God as first priority in their lives.

At the closing of his speech he said, *"I hope when you go to bed at nights, that you put your slippers way under the bed, so when you wake up on mornings, you will have to get on your knees to reach them. While you're down there on your knees, say thank you for life, thank you for grace, thank you for mercy, thank you for humility, thank you for parents, thank you for love, thank you for understanding, thank you for wisdom, thank you for kindness, thank you for peace, thank you for prosperity. Say thank you in advance for what is already yours. True desire in the heart for anything GOOD, is God's proof to you, sent beforehand to indicate what is already yours."*

Anything that you want that is good, you can have.

Claim it

Work hard to get it

When you get it, reach out to someone and help them.

"Each One, Teach One."

We need **PRAYER** to become successful. We need to pray repeatedly and persistently until we receive our answer. If you'll put God first, He will crown your efforts of success.

I have to stay close to God because He already knows my end. You just have to begin.

"Then He spoke a parable to them, that men always ought to pray and not lose heart."
Luke 18:1

Prayer is the answer to your problem today.

Chapter Seven

Ask

What is the main reason that most people don't get what they want in life? ***They don't ask.***

Asking is one of the major parts of success.

How do you get whatever you want? ***Ask.***

A lot of people don't know the art of asking. Ask for what you want and you can have it.

ASK

BELIEVE

RECEIVE

What does asking mean? ***Decide what you want, ask, and receive.***

If you don't ask, you won't receive anything.

The Bible says, "Y*ou have not because you ask not*." Such a simple scripture. You don't really have to be a good worker, be a good asker.

THREE THINGS ON ASKING AND RECEIVING:

1. Asking is the beginning of receiving. Asking starts a unique process mentally and emotionally. And it works.

2. Receiving is not the problem. Receiving is automatic; the problem is *failure* to ask.

3. Receiving is like the ocean. There is *plenty*.

"Success is not in short supply."

Some people go to the ocean with a teaspoon, while others go with a bucket.

DON'T GO TO GOD WITH A TEASPOON. TRADE IN YOUR TEASPOON FOR A BUCKET.

There are two ways to ask:

1. Ask with ***intelligence***. Be crystal clear about what you want. Define and describe what you want. It's very powerful. Goals become like a magnet, they pull you in that direction. The better you describe them the more they pull.

ASK YOURSELF:

What size?

What shape?

What color?

How long?

How tall?

How much?

2. Ask with ***faith***. Believe you could get what you want. When you ask it is given.

"So I say to you, ask, and it will be given to you; seek, and you will find; knock, and it will be opened to you."
Luke 11:9

But at some point you have to stop asking and start expecting. Asking starts the process of receiving. I ask for a lot of things, every day. I'm just expecting to receive more.

You have to be very careful for what you ask for because you just might get it.

Ask for the things that are important in your life. When you ask, you must believe and not doubt. Doubt is a feeling of *uncertainty* or lack of conviction.

What do you want to ask God for? *Whatever you ask for, you can have it.*

- Land

- A house
- A car or cars
- $2,000,000
- A family vacation
- To be closer to God

Whatever it is you can have.

But when you ask...

You have to believe

You have to trust

You got to have faith

You definitely have to work

Don't even think or imagine that you're going to get all these things without working or by waving a magic wand. It's not going to appear out of the sky and land on your lap.

If God is making you wait, be prepared to receive more than what you asked for.

You have to learn to ask before you can act. Too many people are *acting* and <u>not</u> asking for the things they want.

Don't get me wrong, acting and working hard towards success is one of the major keys. But make sure to ask for what you want.

Success is available to all who want it, believe they could have it, and put their plans into actions.

Chapter Eight

Excuses Are Useless

Excuses are for losers.

If you are making excuses, you're wasting time. Whenever you do make excuses, you're hurting yourself.

Why do people make excuses?

"Excuses are rationalization we make to ourselves about people, events, and circumstances. They are invented reasons we create to defend our behavior, to postpone taking action or simply as a means of neglecting responsibility."
~Adam Sicinski

1. Fear of not reaching a goal
2. Fear of hard work
3. Fear of change
4. Fear of success
5. Fear of making mistakes
6. Fear of failure
7. Being scared
8. A belief that life is unfair
9. Lack of confidence
10. Lack of motivation

Living a life of excuses can have dire and lasting consequences. Not only will excuses prevent you from reaching your full potential, but they will also hold you back from recognizing opportunities, strengths, and skills you might have that could help you overcome your life's problems.

Excuses sound best to the person that's making them up.

"An excuse is a lie stuffed with a reason."
~Billy Sunday

Do not use your mistakes as an excuse to give up. If you don't challenge yourself to reach new heights, you will never really know what you're truly capable of.

Excuses are useless.

It prevents you from reaching your potential. When you're relentlessly working on your dreams you shouldn't have anytime to make excuses.

Be so busy focusing on the road to success, the word excuse doesn't even exist in your vocabulary.

WINNERS DON'T MAKE EXCUSES, THEY MAKE ADJUSTMENTS.

You want to be financially independent; you want to own your time and your money? ***STOP MAKING EXCUSES.***

The choice is yours: ***make money*** or ***make excuses***. You cannot do both.

Money goes where it is invited and stays where it is welcomed. Make sure you have that invitation to give.

LET ME INTRODUCE YOU TO THE FOUR **Cs**:

Those Who...

Criticize

Condemn

Complain

Are afraid of **Change**

DEFINITIONS

Criticize: *Indicate the fault of someone in a disapproving way.*

Condemn: *Express complete disapproval; censure.*

Complain: *Express dissatisfaction about something.*

Change: *Make or become something.*

The first three Cs are for the excuse makers: **GET THAT OUT OF YOUR LIFE.**

CONGRATULATIONS to the people who are making a change and to those who have already made that change.

Changes should improve your life, not make it worst.

Why do you want to spend time criticizing, condemning, and complaining?

- To show people how you can stay BROKE for the rest of your life.
- To show people your J.O.B (***Just Over Broke***) is the better thing to do for forty to forty five years and retire broke. After this time has passed, you'd end up looking for another **J.O.B.**

There is nothing to prove to people when you are living your life in the first three Cs. People make dumb excuses for no reason at all.

Here are some examples:

1. Why didn't you read the book? *Because my boss said I can't read it.*

2. How come you didn't attend the business meeting? *I injured my knee and it started to hurt so I didn't wanted to hop to the meeting.*

3. Why didn't you make any phone calls? *My parrot broke out of the cage, stole my phone, and flew away.*

4. Why didn't you sell the product? *Everyone in the world was asleep at 12am. I couldn't sell the product, so I slept as well.*

5. Why didn't you work this month? *I had $300 in my bank account and thought it would've lasted.*

- How much do you have in your bank account now? *Zero.*

ALL these excuses are useless.

And some people wonder why they are stagnant. Excuses keep you from achieving your goals.

I used to make excuses and realized it was futile. I am an independent business owner; I am a network marketing duplicator. In my business I have to help people.

I have two choices: **make excuses** to support those *failing* or be a **role model** for *success.* I choose the latter.

Helping people is a major part of success.

"Success is not defined by how much money you have, but how many people are better off, because you live."
~ Bill Britt.

No one can determine if you'll be successful or not. You are the only one who could determine your destiny; you are in control of making great things happen in your life. Don't allow people who failed at fulfilling their dreams, to stop you from pursuing yours.

You are the director of your movie.

You are the star of your life.

Aim for the stars and reach to the moon.

POSITIVE SPEECH: DAILY AFFIRMATION

NO EXCUSE IS ACCEPTABLE.

"There are three kinds of people in this world: people who make it happen, people who watch what happens, and people who wonder what happened."
~Nicholas Murray Butler

Which one are you?

Choose wisely.

Chapter Nine

It's Your Dream:
Keep Chasing After It

The first level to success is seeing what you want, and then visualizing it. Your goals must be clear. At some point in your life, your dreams are going to come true.

Dreams can take...

MONTHS

ONE YEAR

YEARS

It doesn't happen overnight. You have to keep chasing after your dreams; it's the only way for it to happen.

"The future belongs to those who believe in the beauty of their dreams."
~Eleanor Roosevelt

"Every great dream begins with a dreamer. Always remember, you have within you the strength, the

patience, and the passion to reach for the stars to change the world."

"Where there is no revelation, the people cast off restraint; but happy is he who keeps the law." ~Proverbs 29:18

What does that mean? *Those that don't have dreams, goals, or purpose, will end up somewhere they didn't imagine.*

Vision is the manifestation of your purpose.

So have dreams. The people who walk around aimlessly, has no destination. Having a vision for your life in the next two to five years costs you nothing.

Don't stop dreaming and dream big.

How bad do you want it?

What are you willing to give up to live your dreams?

How hungry are you for your dreams?

Do you know what's scary and painful at the same time? *Not providing for your family the way you would want to.*

My family has to eat. They give me the drive and determination to go out there and get my business done.

Don't lose your dreams. Those dreams you have are for you, your family, and your future.

You have to make sacrifices to make your dreams become a reality.

You have to do whatever it takes to be a champion.

It is **your** dream; don't expect anybody to believe in your dreams like you do. You have to support your dream by moving forward. If you want your dream to come true, **RISE AND GRIND.** You have to discipline yourself to get it done.

You also have to change your old habits into new habits: not just new habits, but successful habits. If you want something you never had, you must be willing to do something you never did. You have to make a concrete decision to start the process to become successful.

Don't even think or say that you will *try*...

NO

NO

NO

Trying is simply to *fail* or <u>not</u> doing anything. It's either you do or you don't. Success is doing what the failures won't do.

Don't leave your dream a dream.

Plan for it

Work for it

Make it your reality

Write your dreams down.

"Write the vision and make it plain on tablets,
that he may run who reads it.
For the vision is yet for an appointed time;
but at the end it will speak, and it will not lie.
Though it tarries, wait for it; because it will surely
come, it will not tarry."
~Habakkuk 2:2-3

What does *tarry* mean? *Take a length of time, to linger in expectation, wait for something.*

How long can you stick around to see your dream become a reality?

Stay steady

Remain humble

Keep on keeping on

Stay persistent and consistent

What is the purpose of writing down your dreams? *It plants the information in your subconscious mind.*

Have a **dream board** or a *dream list*. Read your dream list every morning and every night to keep reminding yourself of your goals.

There are people with small dreams and people with big dreams; the bigger the dream, the bigger the accomplishment.

REALITY CHECK FOR ALL THOSE READING THIS BOOK:

The job that you're working at won't make you rich or wealthy or give you financial independence. **Your parents told you to:**

- *Go to school*
- *Get good grades*
- *Get a job*
- *Work for a boss where the company has good benefits for forty to forty five years*

What is the end result? You retire... ***BROKE!***

At your job you work hard. Why not work hard and smart towards your future? Working at a job is not your dream. I can boldly say this without apology. Your dream is to get involved in business for yourself and live your dreams.

Do you want financial freedom? *Get involved in business for yourself. Surround yourself with people who will help you along the way to achieve your goals.*

Going to your job has become a burden.

TYPICAL WORK DAY

Waking up early on mornings to go to a job you dislike	Seeing people you don't want to see
Working in a toxic environment	Listen to many negative conversations by your coworkers
Hear criticism about your job performance	Listen to coworkers complain about their lives
Depression	Your boss tells you what time to go to and return from lunch

On your job they own a majority of your time and pay you a salary. Your income is limited.

At the job where you work, you make your boss richer. If you do not pursue your dreams, you will work for somebody to pursue theirs.

Get involved in your own business to start the process of accumulating your own wealth and help other people do the same.

I have nothing against working for others, but let your job **prepare** you to get started in your own business. When your business grows to a certain level and you start seeing consistent profit, then you can FIRE your boss. You are very capable of getting this done. You showed up on the earth with a dream; commit yourself to your dreams and goals.

YOU HAVE GREATNESS WITHIN YOU.

Discipline is a major part of success.

When people hear the word discipline, they think it's a punishment. *That's incorrect.*

I define self-discipline by asking these questions:

- What are your daily habits?
- What do you need to make your dream a reality?

Make discipline a priority in your life. Through discipline you can get things done. Discipline is having the ability to push yourself to do the things that are necessary. This is done constantly and becomes a habit. Without self-discipline your dreams would not be possible.

Goals cannot be achieved without discipline.

Do the things you're supposed to do to make your dreams come true, even when you don't feel like doing it.

Do it when you feel discouraged.

Do it when you're under the weather.

Make it a daily habit to focus and commit to your business.

It is said that *a man's reward, for dedication to excellence is not what he gets from it, but who he becomes through it.*

/

Start creating good habits and get rid of the old habits. Shape your mindset towards serious work habits to the road of success. Give 100% of yourself. Take control of your destiny. Disciplining yourself means more freedom.

If your daily routine is not lining up on the path to your success, change it. That's the only way you are going to see results.

"Self-discipline is the center of all material success. You cannot win the war against the world, if you can't win the war against your own mind."

~Will Smith

THE TRUTH ABOUT SUCCESS:

Success is not something that you do; success is something that you become.

Success is doing the things that you are supposed to do which are necessary to become successful.

Success is not a destination, it's a journey.

- Your dream is about becoming a master of your destiny.
- You have to go after your future.
- No one is going to give it to you.
- You can do extraordinary things.
- Start pursuing your purpose.

You aren't going to reach anywhere until you take the first step. You don't need to see the whole staircase, just take the first step.

You have to make a decision that can shape the rest of your life to see your dreams come true.

Success = the result of your ***decisions***.

Failure = the result of your ***decisions***.

Whatever you are, that is what you decided to become. Anything can be achieved. You have to first believe. You have to believe that you can see it.

You make a difference in this world when you become what you're supposed to. You can impact lives when you're living your dream. So start operating like it's your last day on earth and begin to move towards your dreams. You can achieve whatever you want, just be passionate about it.

YOU CAN DO IT.

Don't be affected by the people around you when pursuing your dreams.

Maybe you're not in the right environment or your circumstances are subpar. Just because your family and friends have a different dream, goal, motivation, determination, dedication, and aspiration, it doesn't mean that you should be discouraged.

As I said in chapter 5, you have to identify your **WHY** to give you the courage to push through all your adversities.

You need to have a mentor; you cannot do it on your own.

A mentor:

- Helps you
- Sees your blind spots
- Gives you information for success
- Guides you along the way
- Provides motivation and emotional support
- Is a role model
- Helps you set goals, develop contacts, and identify resources

- Coaches you

A mentor is someone who paved the way for you to succeed. Do you know what you call that?
Monkey see monkey do.

Every day when I pray I ask God for certain things; that He places important people in my life.

I pray

Ask

Wait on God

When I commenced my career as a motivational speaker, I began doing two to three minute videos to post on Facebook. After some time passed, something surprising happened: I received a message on Messenger...

4G
100%
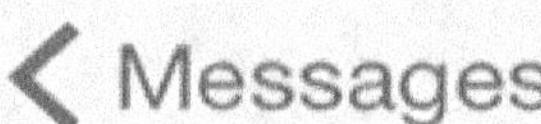
Messages
Robbie
Details
What's up?
I'm great. What's up with you and the family?
We are great.
Nice.
Grateful for greatness.
Awesome.
I see that you are into some heavy motivation.
Yes I am. I'm also writing my first book at the moment.

Text Message
Send

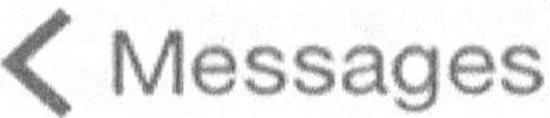

Messages **Robbie** Details

Wow, that's great. Nice.

Where are you? Are you in the country? Robbie, did God tell you to message me? Because you ran across my mind and I see that business is going great for you; there's been a lot of growth.

I was actually picturing myself speaking to some of your business partners, motivating, and encouraging them to be excited about building their business. I just found it strange that you messaged me because we haven't spoken since 2011...

Text Message Send

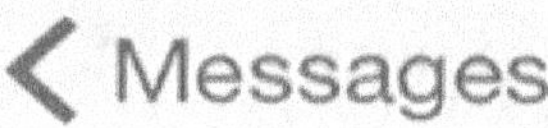

Anyhow, I'm very thankful that you messaged me.

Yea man Damian man, I'm really glad to see that you're doing some inspiring stuff, keep it up. We have to meet sometime because I want to see what you're doing. And you know what I always tell people? "Hands on approach to personal self-development is always the key." I see you're doing that on your own, which is awesome man.

You're probably wondering who Robbie is...

Robbie and his wife are very successful independent business owners, growing their network marketing business throughout Trinidad and Tobago, the Caribbean, and other parts of the world.

Robbie and I met. We discussed business and my desire for him and his wife Shishma, to be our (my wife and me) personal mentors.

A mentor is someone who tells you what you may not want to hear, and help you see what you may not be able to see. They encourage you to become who you always hoped to be.

I'm very excited about that. That was something I'd pray for and ***my prayer was answered***. This is why prayer is important as I told you in an earlier chapter. Just ask and wait on God.

Be humble, have patience, and things would happen the way it's supposed to happen.

You have to expect great things to happen.

Just remember: Your dreams are yours. Hold on to your dreams and don't allow any ***dream stealers*** to deter you.

CALLING ALL MEN AROUND THE WORLD…

Husbands ✓

Men who are about to get married ✓

Men who have intentions of getting married ✓

Husbands: If your wife is at a job, make it your personal duty to get your wife out of that job… FIRE HER BOSS.

Men need to have ***visions*** and ***dreams***.

Find your gift, pursue it, and bring your wife home from that frustrating and stressful place.

That is a big dream to have. A woman was designed to be a man's helper; to make the family dreams become a reality. Husbands are to *lead* and not control their wives. That's what great leaders do, lead by **example**.

MY DEFINITION OF BEING A GREAT MAN:

Fear God

Pray daily and consistently

Work on your gift

Live your purpose

Be an exceptional husband and father

Make sure that your family is happy by living your dream. Protect your dreams from negative things. Keep a picture of your dreams and look at it daily. Stop hanging around negative people.

If anything knocks you down, GET BACK UP!

Never give up on your dream.

A dream is something you carry in your mind; you have to bulletproof your mind. Stay focused on what's ahead of you. You always have to be excited.

DO IT!

DON'T STOP!

Whatever tries to stop you, should fuel your strength.

Chapter Ten

Find Your Work And Work Hard

When I mean work hard, I'm not talking about working hard on the job, I mean working hard on your future.

Always work hard and have fun in what you do. I believe that's when you're more successful. You have to make up your mind to do it.

"Hard work pays off. Hard work beats talent any day. If you're talented and work hard, it's tough to beat.
~Robert Griffin III

Stay positive and happy. Working hard is what successful people do. Nothing comes easy. Doing well comes with a responsibility: hard work. Working hard for what you want shows a sign of discipline.

You must be hungry, with a winner's mindset. You must be willing to do whatever it takes to elevate yourself. In order to get to the next level in life, you have to make a decision to **work**.

If you want to own an immensely elaborate house, drive a luxury vehicle (such as a Benz/BMW/Range Rover), acquire wealth and status, you can't sit around wishing on a lucky charm... **YOU HAVE TO WORK HARD!**

You don't get what you deserve; you get what you work for.

Everybody wants to succeed, but few are willing to work. You have the ability to commit and make decisions. The position you're currently in, is based on decisions you've made in the past.

Decide to work hard on your dreams. We all have a purpose, but hard work is what will pay off.

When you pursue your goals, the end result will surpass your expectations. Your dreams will begin to manifest.

I was a very lazy person before I discovered my gift. I didn't want to work at all and expected things to come to me. I always had a taste for the fine things in life, but I was ***not*** willing to work for it.

There's a saying that goes, *"I wish I can stay at home and money can come knocking on my door."* That was my thinking. **NONSENSE!**

"Good things come to those who wait?" **NO. NO. NO.** Good things come to those who get up and work. Success does not come to those who wait, success comes to those who go out and get it. Good things happen to those who hustle.

We all have innate gifts, but the success from that gift does not just happen. You have to get up and get it.

The reason why some people get what they want in life is because they are *persistent*. What you were born to do is not an easy task, even though it is simple. You have to be persistent and unrelenting.

Success is the reward of hard work and hustle.

Hard work will lead you to success. It's time to begin the process of getting involved and building your own business. After you go home from your job, work on your side hustle. That's what I believe... Actually that's how it is.

Some people have said to themselves, *"I don't need to work, I will just stay at home, pray to God, and He will supply all my needs."*

NO

NO

NO

How could you pray for blessings, but not work? It doesn't happen that way.

You can run across the whole church ✓, jump up and down ✓, sing praises onto God ✓, shout out HALLELUJAH eighty thousand times ✓, but hard work doesn't cross your mind... ***You ain't going to get nothing.***

"In the sweat of your face you shall eat bread..."
~Genesis 3:19

People also have the audacity to say, *"I have faith in God so I don't need to work."*

HILARIOUS!

The Bible says that "*faith without works is dead*".

What does that mean? *If you see what you want and you're not working towards it, you're not going to get it. I hate laziness.*

You have to come out of your comfort zone to see results, get comfortable being uncomfortable.

If you want to succeed you can't expect to just sit around and see things manifest in your life.

Let me get a little deep with you. There is a difference between your job and your work. *Your job is something that you do, and your work is what you are.* You're probably wondering what I mean by that.

DEFINITIONS BY DAMIAN

1. **Job**: where you go to an establishment to work for an employer. They pay you a salary to fulfill **their** future.

2. **Work**: is your God given gift used to fulfill your purpose and accomplish **your** dreams.

"Your work is not your job; your job is what they pay you to do. Your work is what you were born to do."
~Dr. Myles Munroe

Your job is your skills; your work is your gift.

You can get fired from your job; no one can fire you from your work (your gift).

The word **work** means to *become, reveal, manifest, or fulfill.* It means to discover and become what you were born to be through self-manifestation.

You and I are not supposed to go to work; you're supposed to manifest work. So you have already seen your vision of knowing what you're supposed to become. You were created by God to discover your work.

No matter what people may try to do, **YOU WILL SUCCEED**.

Success is the fulfillment of purpose.

Purpose > is determined by the gift

Your gift > fulfills your purpose

It is important to find your work because that's the only way you are going to succeed. I am enjoying my *work*. It feels great when you have found your purpose and pursue it.

Your gifts have a lot of value.

Your job has limits. They pay you a fixed amount of money (at the end of every week/fourth nightly/monthly). If you ask for an increase in your salary, your boss tells you, *"let me think about it."*

At your job they pay you what the job is worth, they don't pay you what you are worth.

There are no limitations to your work. You can pay yourself any amount of money you want.

- You are the director and CEO of your own business.

- You are in charge of how much money you can make.

- Don't put limits on yourself.

- You are limitless.

Unlock your unlimited potential to begin the process to reach your destination. Don't be afraid to activate your potential to succeed.

Limited thinking *affects unlimited potential*.

Open up your mind and change your mindset. You must change your "should" into must.

If you're stuck only ***thinking*** about your dreams, it will never happen. You have to believe that you will accomplish your dreams.

You must have a strong work ethic. Your work ethic determines your level of success. Your work ethic must be goal oriented; you won't even have time to procrastinate.

I used to procrastinate a lot, putting off things towards my business and telling myself, *"Damian you know what, you can leave that thing you're supposed to do today for tomorrow."*

Do you know what happens when you procrastinate?

Tomorrow ends up being another tomorrow.

↓

Then that tomorrow ends up being next week.

Next week ends up being next month.

Next month ends up being next year.

Next year ends up being years.

If you don't act now, you will remain stuck. Sometimes you might want to put off your business to go hang out with some friends at a bar, or any kind of useless environment... These all keep you back from working towards your dream.

Every minute counts.

To me, a true friend is someone who will help you work towards your dreams. If someone says they are your friend and they are not contributing to your growth in business or your success, they are your enemy.

Decisions determine success.

POWER OF THE SEVEN Ps

PURPOSE

POTENTIAL

PASSION

PLAN

PEOPLE

PERSISTENT

PRINCIPLES

1. **Purpose**: *is the reason for which something is done or created or for which something exists.*

Purpose is the original intent for creation. There is no way that you're going to be successful unless you have a clear guiding purpose. Your purpose is a clear vision for the reason why you exist. There is a reason why you were born; a reason why you were given life by the Creator.

You were created to achieve something that no one else can. Once your purpose is clear you are going to be successful. **Working on a job collecting a salary was never your purpose.** That job is a temporary thing.

2. **Potential**: *is having the capacity to develop into something in the future.*

Potential is the inherent ability to fulfill purpose. It is what you can do.

3. **<u>Passion</u>**: *is a very strong feeling about something or a strong belief in something.*

Passion is a commitment that is beyond contention. This means that if anything tries to stop you from pursuing your dreams, it will fail. A person with passion always stands out.

4. **<u>Plan</u>**: *a detailed proposal for doing or achieving something.*

Write down your plans. Whatever you see in your vision put it on paper. Planning is a command from God. God will direct your steps if you have a plan. If you do not have a plan God has nothing to direct.

If you fail to plan, you plan to fail.

5. **<u>People</u>**: *you cannot be successful without people.*

However, you have to be careful of the people you put in your life. Your success is based upon how many people are better off because you live.

6. **Persistent**: *unrelenting; a consistent pursuance.*

You refuse to stop. Nobody can stop you from accomplishing your goals.

7. **Principle**: *a fundamental truth or proposition that serves as the foundation for a system of belief.*

Principles are the inherent laws.

In my line of business, I've come to realize that the potential you have within needs to be released to fulfill your purpose. It is followed by success principles. There are success principles that are already laid out for you to follow. You don't need to reinvent the wheel to success.

Why? *There are people who've already accomplished their goals by following the principles of success.*

The principles are designed for you to succeed. You cannot fail once you follow them. If you don't follow, you will fail.

Purpose produces potential.

I use my work as a business opportunity; I share with people. I know what I'm doing. My mentors have been coaching me through the process, encouraging me to create a game plan and work.

If you are struggling financially, listen up... I can choose who I want to do business with. I don't have time for procrastinators and negative people that have no desire to succeed.

I rather facts over the opinions of others.

What is a fact? **A description of the present state of things; a thing that is known or proven to be true.**

A principle is an eternal truth; it is a set truth, which means it is fixed.

What is an opinion? **A view or judgement formed about something, not necessarily based on fact or knowledge.**

For example: I share my business opportunity with people, go through the whole process of launching your business, and here comes one of your negative friends or family members telling you about my business (that they don't even know about)... They try to discourage you from pursuing your purpose.

I want you to know this: if someone is telling you about something and they are not doing it, don't listen to them. They're not an expert.

- If you want to know how to fix a problem in your car, visit your mechanic.

- If want to know how to fix a leak in your pipe, call your plumber.

- If you have an electrical issue, visit your electrician.

If you want to be rich, wealthy, or financially independent, you must listen to the people who are doing it and those who have already done it.

Someone who is struggling financially (or in other words **BROKE**), cannot teach you on how to become a multi-millionaire. Someone who's broke could only teach you on how to be broke.

BROKE PEOPLE CANNOT HELP BROKE PEOPLE.

This is not rocket science. Be around people who will help you with your financial future. If you want to be successful, find someone who has achieved the results you want, copy what they do, and you will achieve the same results.

I have found my work and I'm doing it. I'm very passionate and know that I have to work hard.

No more mediocrity

No more poverty

No more suffering

No more pain

You must be passionate when you are working on your goals and dreams. Passion is *energy* that is created by a **purpose** and meaningful life. It also means that it is a commitment that is beyond contention.

Anything that comes against you cannot stop you from accomplishing your dreams.

When you're passionate about working to achieve your dreams, it becomes a reality.

When you have passion towards the thing you are obligated to, you forget to eat; sometimes you forget to take a shower. Sometimes you miss sleep.

Just remember when you have passion, nothing or no one can stop you.

Every successful person has worked hard to achieve their goals. If you think that you're going to achieve something huge, or be great in anything, and believe you can do it without working, you are wrong. No matter what you do, you've got to work hard to get it done. If you're not willing to work hard, **forget about it**.

It is very important that you put in the hard work to achieve your dreams.

"In order to achieve greatness or to begin the process to accumulate wealth, you have to be willing to do the things today that others won't do, in order to have the things tomorrow that others won't have."
~ Les Brown

Sometimes I have sleepless nights because I'm hungry, thirsty, and excited about success. I know the sacrifices I have to make and the hard work I have to put in to create my success.

Whatever you are aiming for, you can achieve it. Don't set the bar on a low level!

A quote about discipline by Jocko Willink states,
"...it requires hard work, late nights, early mornings, practice, repetition, studying, sweat, blood, toil, and discipline..."

Discipline overcomes laziness.

You must have discipline. You can definitely do it! There are no shortcuts, just make it happen. Good choices will always position you in life to win.

I've watched a lot of interviews with Kobe Bryant, one of the greatest NBA players in history. One of his quotes about hard work stood out to me: "*The best way to prove your value is to work, to learn, to absorb, to be a sponge. You always want to out work your potential. As hard as you can believe that you can work, you can work harder than that.*"

The only way for you to be the best or be a master at what you do is to practice and work every day.

I understand that no matter what challenges or circumstances may come my way, I have to keep going. I always have to keep pushing.

Remember, pain and struggles are temporary. Push through the storm, eventually the storm will settle.

Always do your best, but never feel that you're better than anyone.

This is what is needed to achieve success.

Put in the work to achieve greatness because that is what you were born to do.

Chapter Eleven

The Struggles Are Real

I was born on October 22, 1984, at the Eric Williams Medical Science Complex in Trinidad and Tobago. My parents are Gloria and Peter Hernandez. My mother has always been a very hard working lady. The most important priority for her was taking care of me and my two sisters (Denise and Rhona). My father seldom provided for us financially.

My mother struggled to take care of us and pay the bills. However, she always made sure that my sisters and I had three square meals.

Children don't ever have anything to worry about. They don't have bills, rent or a mortgage to pay. Their main concern is food, clothing, and toys. They don't even know how hard their parents work to ensure their happiness. *Many of us shared this experience.*

I've had a great taste of this life when I was younger.

I also have two other sisters who live in the United States; they both have different fathers. I am the youngest of five: **four** girls and *one* boy.

I am a spoiled brat.

The first time I visited the US, I was six years old. My mother saved her small salary (along with the help of my eldest sisters: Gemma and Marscia) for about a year so she can purchase plane tickets for us to go to Philadelphia on vacation.

Even though my mother was struggling financially, she always used to make sure that her children were happy. I admire that most about her; everything that she's done for us. ***Such a hard worker.***

Whenever she cooked lunch to sell during the week, or had a barbecue/curry cue, I was on the grill. She did all this just to make sure that she had extra cash after the mortgage and bills were paid.

My dad used to help somewhat with the bills. He was a taxi driver and went about his daily routine, ***trying his best to survive.***

I attended school in Trinidad: Arima Centenary Government Primary School, Arima New Government Primary School, and then St. Charles High School in Tunapuna, which was a private school at that time.

My mother had to pay my school fee of $700.00TT every term. No matter what, she made sure she paid this school fee. When she couldn't afford it, she borrowed money from people. She was given a few days ***grace period*** after the deadline to pay, but if not, I couldn't attend school.

If they gave her a week to get the money, my mother would take an entire month to find that cash, but somehow she got the money borrowed. While she looked for the money, she had to call or go to the school to ensure my attendance.

In the midst of all of this, utility bills came, especially the electricity bill (which was due for disconnection).

One day, I came home from school, went into the refrigerator to get some juice and the light didn't come on when I opened it. I looked at the microwave to see the time, but it was off; I thought someone unplugged it.

I went to the living room to put the fan and the television on… **NOTHING**. I thought perhaps the entire neighborhood was in darkness. So I just waited for it to come back.

When my mother arrived, I said to her, "Electricity went out and it should come back on anytime now."

"Are you sure?" she asked.

"Yes, I believe so," I replied.

It was getting late, as the sun was going down and the night started to enter. Surprisingly, every house in the neighborhood had electricity, but our house was shrouded in darkness.

That was a very embarrassing situation, because it was the **ONLY** house in the neighborhood with no lights.

I mentally prepared myself... If anyone asked why the house had no lights, I would just tell them that it's an **electrical problem**.

Mummy had no money to pay the electricity bill, so she had a friend, who is a handyman, put the lights back on without Trinidad & Tobago Electricity Control (T&TEC) knowing anything.

You can't do that anymore because of technological advancement.

My father continued to work as a taxi driver, but barely contributed to the household expenses. The stress took a toll on my mother, she became frustrated.

I would look at my mother doing what she had to do to make sure she paid the household expenses. She borrowed money, did lunches by orders (only in the week), had a barbecue or curry-cue on the weekends and somehow got money to buy a plane ticket to go to America.

She'd buy clothes and accessories, come back to Trinidad and sell them. All of this **just to pay bills**, make sure we had food, and the finances needed to pay the taxi driver when she went to work.

Mom was a go getter, actually she still is. I owe my mother a lot, but the mere fact is I can't really give to her the way she gave to me. Even at 71, she still does things for me.

/

Growing up, my father was physically and verbally abusive to my mother. After he came home from work, he would always have arguments with mom. His excuse would always be why he couldn't help with the bills. *"I'm not making enough money on the road."*

Whenever he did help my mom with the bills, he was left with some money to put gas in the car for the next day. He never began the day with a float to give his passengers change.

My father was also an addict; he used to smoke marijuana. He had affairs with women. For years he was doing that crap, and my mom knew and she still stayed with him.

When my mother went to America it was just my father, my sisters, and I, left at home. He used to sneak women into the house and my sisters and I pretended we didn't know what was going on.

I remember one time, I went into my parents room and my father said, "Stop, don't enter the room now."

I found it strange because it was a normal thing for me to go into their room unannounced. I didn't pay him any mind when he said that.

Right behind my parents' door was a cupboard for their clothes. There was a curtain in front of the cupboard. Suddenly, I saw the curtain moving... I swear it had a zombie behind the curtain.

So I slammed the door onto the curtain and heard a lady scream out, "OH LOOOORD."

Immediately she scampered out of the room and he had to leave to take her wherever he picked her up from.

On another occasion with that same lady, my sister Denise, who was pregnant at the time, caught her outside of the house hiding behind some wall. My sister ran the lady down with her big belly.

I was like, "Why were you running down this woman and you're pregnant? Did she take something from you?"

Thank God nothing serious happened to my sister or her baby.

Things with my father began to get worst.

He was introduced to cocaine by a woman he was probably having an affair with. I found my father was acting real strange, the way he moved. He began to hallucinate and asked me if I saw what he was seeing.

One time he came into my room, shifted the curtain to look outside of the window and asked me, "*Who is that man sitting on the mango tree outside there?"*

I stared at him. "*Who man are you talking about?"*

"*The man out there, he's sitting on the mango tree looking at me."* He became frightened. "*Come to see the man I'm talking about."*

When I looked outside, I saw no one.

The funny thing about this scene? It was nighttime when he came into my room. You couldn't see the mango tree.

"*How are you seeing somebody in the dark?"* I asked.

"Look the man is right there pointing at me."

I watched my dad. "*Are you crazy?"*

He left my room in distress.

This strange behavior went on for many nights. He had me wondering who the man was that he kept on seeing outside.

The worst was not over.

I remember the time I came home from school and things were missing in the house.

No television

No microwave

No toaster oven

My new Nike sneakers... ***GONE***

My jewelry... ***GONE***

The list goes on...

Someone broke into the house. Guess who it was? ***MY FATHER.***

You wouldn't believe this; he also called the police to make a report.

I really thought we got robbed.

He wanted the drugs so bad, that he was using his salary, money from the furniture he sold, plus some of my things, to buy the drugs.

It started to get really out of hand and my mother was **sick** and **tired** of his foolishness. My mother decided without hesitation that she was going to remove herself from the house. My sisters and I went with her.

We left him there because he was turning the house upside down.

This was very messed up and painful for us. We had to leave our house which was almost paid for, to go find a place to rent.

So we left and got a place to rent. We left the majority of our stuff at the house and mom had to start over. My dad turned our home into a crack house because of his addiction to drugs.

We had to move about three times to make sure we got a comfortable place to stay.

We're in a comfortable place now.

No matter what you do in life you will face some kind of struggle or pain. If you want to share your story with people, you have to go through the struggles;

you can't give people a testimony without going through the test.

Nobody wants to hear a story from someone that had everything handed to them on a ***silver platter***.

LEARN TO FORGIVE

In spite of the mistakes my dad made, I forgave him and moved on with life. If I didn't forgive him, I would have poisoned my spirit.

"Let all bitterness, wrath, anger, clamor, and evil speaking be put away from you, with all malice. And be kind to one another, tenderhearted, forgiving one another, even as God in Christ forgave you."
Ephesians 4:31-32

My father is a better man today, thanks to God. He got over his drug addiction. He could have been living on the street and eating out of trash cans. Through the drug rehab center and prayers, he made it, and ***recovered***. I love my father and he is a man of God, knowing the importance of having Jesus Christ as his personal Lord and savior. My dad is doing great.

LEAVE YOUR PAST IN THE PAST

If you're holding on to something that happened to you in the past, you need to leave it behind.

Leave your past in the past, because if you allow your past to dictate your future you won't go anywhere.

If someone hurt you or you hurt them, know that God has a bright future for you.

"Do not remember the former things, nor consider the things of old. Behold, I will do a new thing, now it shall spring forth; shall you not know it? I will even make a road in the wilderness and rivers in the desert."

Isaiah 43:18-19

"Therefore, if anyone is in Christ, he is a new creation; old things have passed away; behold, all things have become new."
2 Corinthians 5:17

Leaving the past behind is basically *shaking off the dead weight and leaving it right where it is*.

Don't bring the past along with you because it won't serve you any good in the present.

Stop allowing what you did yesterday to define your future. Leave your past behind so you can focus on your future.

Whatever happened in your past cannot be changed. *Holding on to something you can't change is insanity.* So let it go because your past doesn't define you, it refines you.

Holding on to the hurt someone caused you, prevents you from reaching your goals. While you are holding on to whatever that person has done to you, they've already moved on with life. They're achieving greatness. The best **revenge** is to move on with your life. Move on to the next positive, drop the negative, and focus on what you can do today.

LET IT GO and live your life fully.

Chapter Twelve

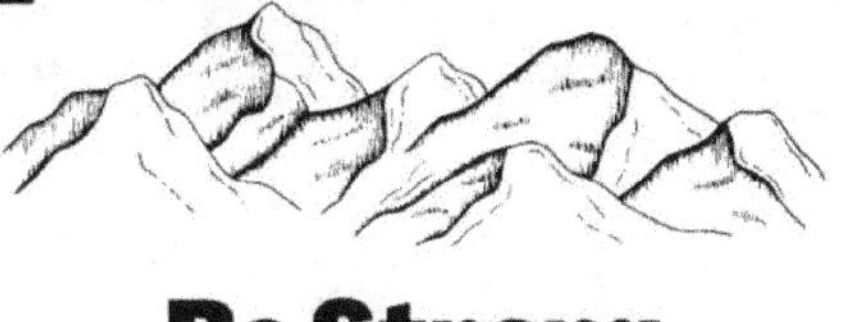

Be Strong

It's time to stand up for what you believe in.

The struggles that we go through in our lives, is not supposed to make us feel weak. The adversities we face are supposed to make us stronger. Too many people give up on life easily because of challenges. You cannot run away from it. You've just got to embrace it, it is going to come, and you have to be ready for it.

The tough situations are going to take you to new levels. Once you have the right mindset of:

- Knowing what you want
- Speaking what you want
- Fearlessness
- Faith
- Winning
- Prayer

- Being diligent; not making any excuses
- Running the course
- Working hard

You're going to be faced with obstacles.

Be Serious

Strong

Passionate

Bold

Being strong, is when you grow in the moments when you think you can't go on but you keep going anyway. Whenever you find yourself doubting how far you can go, just remember how far you've come.

Remember your experiences, the battles you won, and all the fears you overcame.

You were given this life because you are strong enough to live it.

You have to know success is yours; no one can take it from you. It is yours to fight for.

There is going to be a time in your life where you have to push through your pain. This is going to be a test for you; it can either break you, or make you.

When you are faced with obstacles, it'll make you stronger. Every struggle that you are going through, God is preparing you for GREATNESS.

When you push through pain you will be stronger.

When you push through pain that's when you bring out your greatness.

You have to be a lion when you're going after your dream.

Your mind has to be strong.

Your words have to be strong.

Your body has to be strong.

You have to have strong dreams.

Without struggles there will be no victory.
It is not over until you win.

Develop that strength you have because you will definitely win. It's just a matter of time before your dreams come true.

In life you will go through a lot of hurt and pain, but you have to be strong and understand the reason why God sent you on earth. Nothing in life was ever meant to be easy; it's about going through the test to share your testimony.

You have to be at your strongest when you're feeling at your weakest.

Being strong doesn't mean you'll never get hurt. It means even when you get hurt, you'll never let it defeat you. No matter what, you'll still be criticized. People will say negative things about you, when you're doing great. They will even say things about you that are not true.

When all of this happens, know that you're important. You are doing something great for the envious people to talk about. They're spending time minding your business instead of minding theirs. If people take that same time and *energy* to focus on their business, they will definitely succeed.

Your life is yours.

It's time to take control of it.

It's time to be that person God created you to be.

It's time to take action, show people how strong you are.

Step out and be great. In order to achieve greatness you first have to believe you can.

- Push through the pressure.
- Push through the pain.
- Push through the struggles.
- Push through the depression.
- Push through the lazy days.

You know why? Because...

YOU WERE BORN GREAT!

GO OUT IN THIS WORLD TO WIN AND FULFILL YOUR PURPOSE.

You want to move forward in your life? Change your mindset and make the right choices. Your brain is very powerful. There are two sides of the brain, in five different ways:

- Good Side	- Bad Side
- Correct Side	- Wrong Side
- Positive Side	- Negative Side
- Righteous Side	- Unrighteous Side
- God	- Devil

ONLY YOU HAVE THE POWER TO TAKE RESPONSIBILITY TO MOVE FORWARD IN YOUR LIFE.

MAKE THE RIGHT DECISION.

DAMIAN'S BOOK
RECOMMENDATIONS

1. Beyond Positive Thinking by Dr. Robert Anthony
2. Born To Be Rich by Rollan A. Roberts II
3. Change It! by Bill Quain and Doug Price
4. How To Think Like A Millionaire by Mark Fisher and Marc Allen
5. Hung By The Tongue by Francis P. Martin
6. The Gift of Attitude by Sam Glenn
7. The Magic of Thinking Big by David J. Schwartz
8. Think and Grow Rich by Napoleon Hill
9. Today Matters by John C. Maxwell
10. Ultimate Productivity by Jim Stovall

BIBLIOGRAPHY

1. Above Inspiration (2017). *Put God First - Denzel Washington. Motivational & Inspiring Commencement Speech* [Video]. https://www.youtube.com/watch?v=BxY_eJLBflk

2. All Christian Quotes (n.d.) Billy Sunday Quotes. Retrieved December 14, 2020 from https://www.allchristianquotes.org/quotes/Billy_Sunday/378/

3. AZ Quotes (n.d.) Les Brown Quotes. Retrieved December 14, 2020, from https://www.azquotes.com/quote/1316059

4. AZ Quotes (n.d.). Martin Luther King Jr. Quotes. Retrieved December 14, 2020, from https://www.azquotes.com/quote/381528

5. Brainy Quote (n.d.) Kobe Bryant Quotes. Retrieved December 14, 2020, from https://www.brainyquote.com/quotes/kobe_bryant_574704

6. Brainy Quote (n.d.) Robert Griffin III Quotes. Retrieved December 14, 2020, from https://www.brainyquote.com/quotes/robert_griffin_iii_504019

7. Brainy Quote (n.d.) Joyce Meyer Quotes. Retrieved December 14, 2020, from https://www.brainyquote.com/quotes/joyce_meyer_565139

8. Carmichael, E. (2018). No Matter How Hard You Work, You Can GO HARDER! – Kobe Bryant Top 10 Rules [Video]. https://www.youtube.com/watch?v=6PDCnhNc2QI

9. Daily Motion (2018) Run After Your Destiny. Bishop TD Jakes Edifying God's People [Video]. https://www.dailymotion.com/video/x6cwtim

10. Fisher, M, and Allen, M (1997). *Think Like A Millionaire*. Novato, CA: New World Library.

11. Harris, S.J. (1968). *Leaving The Surface*. Boston, MA: Houghton Mifflin.

12. Hill, N. (2005). *Think and Grow Rich*. New York, NY: TarcherPerigee.

13. Munroe, M. (2011). *Maximizing Your Potential*. Shippensburg, PA: Destiny Image.

14. Pinterest (n.d.) Bill Britt Quotes. Retrieved December 14, 2020 from https://www.pinterest.com/pin/47710077278452879/

15. Sicinski, A. (2020). *ARE YOU LIVING A LIFE OF ENDLESS EXCUSES? HERE'S HOW TO STOP!* IQ Matrix. https://blog.iqmatrix.com/a-life-of-excuses

16. Whatever It Takes Motivation. (2018, March 2). Will Smith Quotes. Discipline Your Mind. http://www.whateverittakesmotivation.com/2018/03/02/discipline-mind-will-smith-full-speech/

17. Willink, J. (2017). *Discipline Equals Freedom (Field Manual).* New York, NY: St. Martin's Press.

www.ingramcontent.com/pod-product-compliance
Lightning Source LLC
LaVergne TN
LVHW050637100826
845148LV00011B/1890

* 9 7 8 1 7 3 3 8 2 9 3 6 6 *